EFFECTIVE PRESENTATION SKILLS

Steve Mandel

CRISP PUBLICATIONS, INC.
Los Altos, California

EFFECTIVE PRESENTATION SKILLS

Steve Mandel

CREDITS
Editor: **Michael G. Crisp**
Designer: **Carol Harris**
Typesetting: **Interface Studio**
Cover Design: **Carol Harris**
Artwork: **Ralph Mapson**

Copyright © 1987 by Steve Mandel
Printed in the United States of America

Library of Congress Catalog Card Number 86-72078
Mandel, Steve
Effective Presentation Skills
ISBN 0-931961-24-6

PREFACE

The study of how to give effective speeches dates back to ancient Greece. Around 350 B.C. Aristotle wrote his famous *Rhetoric*, now considered to be one of the first formal books on the subject. Now 2,300 years later, we are still struggling with the same problems the Greeks encountered and that speakers have struggled with throughout the ages.

The advent of technology has both complicated and simplified the task of the speaker. For example, today it is possible to produce complex graphs on a computer that will, in turn, produce overhead transparencies. But how much information should we put on that graph? And, most important, where does that graph fit into the organizational plan (if there is one) of the speech?

Effective Presentation Skills attempts to answer the fundamental questions of how to prepare and deliver an effective speech. Proven techniques are presented that will give a reader the necessary skills to give more confident, enthusiastic and persuasive presentations. Topics such as: how to use body language effectively; how to organize thoughts and data for maximum impact; how to develop and use visual aids, as well as (of course) how to deliver what you have prepared.

This book provides some theory but more often presents simple and practical suggestions on how to give more effective presentations.

ABOUT THIS BOOK

EFFECTIVE PRESENTATION SKILLS is not like most books. It has a unique "self-paced" format that encourages a reader to become personally involved. Designed to be "read with a pencil", there are abundant exercises, activities, assessments and cases that invite participation.

The objective of this book is to help a person organize, plan and deliver an effective presentation to others.

THIS BOOK (and the other self-improvement titles listed on page 61) can be used effectively in a number of ways. Here are some possibilities:

—Individual Study. Because the book is self-instructional, all that is needed is a quiet place, some time and a pencil. Completing the activities and exercises will provide valuable feedback, as well as practical ideas for self-improvement.

—Workshops and Seminars. This book is ideal for use during, or as pre-assigned reading prior to a workshop or seminar. With the basics in hand, the quality of participation will improve. More time can be spent practicing concept extensions and applications during the program.

—College Programs. Thanks to the format, brevity and low cost, this book is ideal for short courses and extension programs.

There are other possibilities that depend on the objectives of the user. One thing for sure, even after it has been read, this book will serve as excellent reference material which can be easily reviewed.

TO THE READER

There is a myth that great speakers are born, ''not made,'' that somehow certain individuals have the innate ability to stand in front of an audience with no anxiety, and give a moving, dynamic speech. Well, that just isn't so!

People we consider great speakers usually have spent years developing and practicing their skill. They had to start at the beginning and learn the basics of organization, preparation, delivery and dealing with anxiety. Once the basics were in hand they had to continue to build their abilities.

Professional athletes constantly practice the basics because they know that without such practice they will not survive. To an outsider, the thought of a professional golfer (for example) spending hour upon hour practicing the basics may seem ridiculous. But to that professional, the mastery of those basic skills are the very foundation of success.

Learning to be a better speaker is similar to learning any activity. In the beginning it can be frustrating. After a few lessons where you learn some theory and practice some of the basic skills, things usually improve. To really learn to do anything well takes constant practice and a mastery of the basics.

Speaking is no different. Before becoming comfortable as a speaker you need to learn some basic skills and then actively seek places to practice those skills. This may mean walking into your manager's office and volunteering to give more presentations, or joining a speaking club which allows you to speak in an organized setting. The more experience you gain, the more proficient and comfortable you will become.

Good luck!
Steve Mandel

DEFINITIONS

The terms "speech" and "presentation" are often used interchangeably. For our purposes it is useful to understand the difference.

A presentation is a type of speech. Typically, when we think of a speech we think of a dedication speech, a political speech, a speech of tribute or some similar event that is more public in nature than a presentation would be.

Presentations are speeches that are usually given in a business, technical, professional or scientific environment. The audience is likely to be more specialized than those attending a typical speech event.

Although the difference between speeches and presentations is slight, this book leans toward helping those who give presentations. But, because a presentation is a type of speech, there are ideas and skills in this book that will also be helpful to any speech-maker.

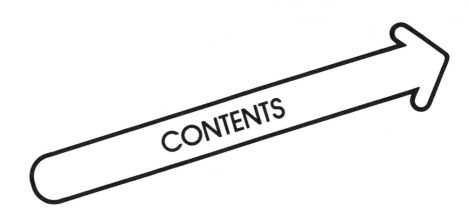

CONTENTS

TABLE OF CONTENTS

SECTION I: ASSESS YOUR SKILLS

EVALUATE YOURSELF

Check the category that best describes you as a speaker:

Category   Characteristics

_____ **AVOIDER**

An avoider does everything possible to escape from having to get in front of an audience. In some cases avoiders may seek careers that do not involve making presentations.

_____ **RESISTOR**

A resistor has fear when asked to speak. This fear may be strong. Resistors may not be able to avoid speaking as part of their job, but they never encourage it. When they do speak they do so with great reluctance and considerable pain.

_____ **ACCEPTOR**

The acceptor will give presentations as part of the job but doesn't seek those opportunities. Acceptors occasionally give a presentation and feel like they did a good job. They even find that once in a while they are quite persuasive, and enjoy speaking in front of a group.

_____ **SEEKER**

A seeker looks for opportunities to speak. The seeker understands that anxiety can be a stimulant which fuels enthusiasm during a presentation. Seekers work at building their professional communication skills and self-confidence by speaking often.

PRESENT PRESENTATION SKILLS SELF-EVALUATION

To be a more effective presenter it is useful to examine your present skills. The following evaluation can help determine the areas on which to focus to increase your competency. Please read the statement and then circle the number that best describes you. Then concentrate during the balance of this book on those items you marked 1, 2 or 3.

	Always				**Never**
1. I determine some basic objectives before planning a presentation.	5	4	3	2	1
2. I analyze the values, needs and constraints of my audience.	5	4	3	2	1
3. I write down some main ideas first, in order to build a presentation around them.	5	4	3	2	1
4. I incorporate both a preview and review of the main ideas as my presentation is organized.	5	4	3	2	1
5. I develop an introduction that will catch the attention of my audience and still provide the necessary background information.	5	4	3	2	1
6. My conclusion refers back to the introduction and, if appropriate, contains a call-to-action statement.	5	4	3	2	1
7. The visual aids I use are carefully prepared, simple, easy to read, and have impact.	5	4	3	2	1
8. The number of visual aids will enhance, not detract, from my presentation.	5	4	3	2	1
9. If my presentation is persuasive, arguments are used that are logical and that support my assertions.	5	4	3	2	1
10. I use anxiety to fuel the enthusiasm of my presentation, not hold me back.	5	4	3	2	1
11. I insure the benefits suggested to my audience are clear and compelling.	5	4	3	2	1
12. I communicate ideas with enthusiasm.	5	4	3	2	1
13. I rehearsed so there is a minimum focus on notes and maximum attention paid to my audience.	5	4	3	2	1

PRESENT PRESENTATION SKILLS SELF-EVALUATION (Continued)

	Always				Never
14. My notes contain only "key words" so I avoid reading from a manuscript.	5	4	3	2	1
15. My presentations are rehearsed standing up and using visual aids.	5	4	3	2	1
16. I prepare answers to anticipated questions, and practice responding to them.	5	4	3	2	1
17. I arrange seating (if appropriate) and check audio-visual equipment in advance of the presentation.	5	4	3	2	1
18. I maintain good eye contact with the audience at all times.	5	4	3	2	1
19. My gestures are natural and not constrained by anxiety.	5	4	3	2	1
20. My voice is strong and clear and is not a monotone.	5	4	3	2	1

Total score _____

If you scored between 80-100, you are an accomplished speaker who simply needs to maintain basic skills through practice.

If your total score was between 60-80, you have the potential to become a highly effective presenter.

If you score was between 40 and 60, this book can help you significantly.

If you scored between 30 and 40, you should show dramatic improvement with practice.

If your total was below 30, roll up your sleeves and dig in. It may not be easy- but you can make excellent progress if you try.

At the conclusion of this program, take this evaluation again and compare your scores. You should be pleased with the progress you have made.

SET SOME GOALS

If your score on the previous page was:

90–100   You have the qualities of an excellent presenter.

70–89   You are above average but could improve in some areas.

Below 69   This program should help you.

WHAT GOALS DO YOU WANT TO ACHIEVE?

Using the information from the self-evaluation form on pages 4 and 5, check those boxes that indicate goals that you would like to achieve:

I hope to:

☐ understand the anxiety I feel before a presentation and learn how to use it constructively during my presentation.

☐ learn how to organize my thoughts and data in a logical and concise manner.

☐ develop the necessary skills to communicate enthusiasm about the ideas I present, and develop a more dynamic presentation style.

☐ transform question-and-answer sessions into an enjoyable and productive part of the presentation process.

☐ construct visual aids that have impact, and use them effectively during my presentation.

SECTION II: DEALING WITH ANXIETY

Anxiety is a natural state that exists any time we are placed under stress. Giving a presentation normally will cause some stress. When this type of stress occurs, physiological changes take place that may cause symptoms such as a nervous stomach, sweating, tremors in the hands and legs, accelerated breathing, and/or increased heart rate.

Don't worry! If you have any of these symptoms before or during a presentation you are normal. If none of these things happen you are one in a million. Almost everyone experiences some stress before presentations, even when the task is something simple like, ''tell the group something about yourself.'' The trick is to make your excess energy work for you.

When you learn to make stress work for you, it can be the fuel for a more enthusiastic and dynamic presentation. The next few pages will teach you how to recycle your stress in a positive form that will help you become a better presenter.

As someone once said, ''the trick is to get those butterflies in your stomach to all fly in one direction!''

DEALING WITH ANXIETY (Continued)

> **Leo** is an engineer with an electronics firm. In two weeks he has to deliver a major presentation to managers from several divisions, on a project he is proposing. He knows his topic, but his audience will be examining his proposal very closely, and Leo is certain he will receive some very tough questions. Every time Leo thinks about planning what to say, he gets too nervous to begin work.

If Leo's problem of anxiety before a presentation sounds familiar then the following may help:

TIPS FOR REDUCING ANXIETY

1. *ORGANIZE*

Lack of organization is one of the major causes of anxiety. Later in this book you will learn a simple technique for organizing your presentation. Knowing that your thoughts are well organized will give you more confidence, which will allow you to focus energy into your presentation.

2. *VISUALIZE*

Imagine walking into a room, being introduced, delivering your presentation with enthusiasm, fielding questions with confidence and leaving the room knowing you did a great job. Mentally rehearse this sequence with all the details of your particular situation, and it will help you focus on what you need to do to be successful.

3. *PRACTICE*

Many speakers rehearse a presentation mentally or with just their lips. Instead, you should practice standing up, as if an audience were in front of you, and use your visual aids (if you have them.) At least two dress rehearsals are recommended. If possible, have somebody critique the first one and/or have it videotaped. Watch the playback, listen to the critique and incorporate any changes you feel are required before your final practice session. *There is no better preparation than this.*

DEALING WITH ANXIETY (Continued)

> **Carol** is an account executive with a software company. She has been asked to present the sales figures for her region at the company's national sales meeting. Her colleague Jack is finishing his remarks and in two minutes she will have to stand up and make her presentation. She is experiencing extreme anxiety at a time when she needs to be focused and collected.

Carol's situation is quite common. If you experience anxiety immediately before speaking, try some of the following exercises next time you're waiting for your turn to stand up and speak:

4. *BREATHE*

When your muscles tighten and you feel nervous, you may not be breathing deeply enough. The first thing to do is to sit up, erect but relaxed, and inhale deeply a number of times.

5. *FOCUS ON RELAXING*

Instead of thinking about the tension---focus on relaxing. As you breathe, tell yourself on the inhale, "I am" and on the exhale, "relaxed." Try to clear your mind of everything except the repetition of the "I am-relaxed" statement and continue this exercise for several minutes.

6. *RELEASE TENSION*

As tension increases and your muscles tighten, nervous energy can get locked into the limbs. This unreleased energy may cause your hands and legs to shake. Before standing up to give a presentation, it is a good idea to try to release some of this pent up tension by doing a simple, unobtrusive isometric exercise.

Starting with your toes and calf muscles, tighten your muscles up through your body finally making a fist (i.e. toes, feet, calves, thighs, stomach, chest, shoulders, arms and fingers). Immediately release all of the tension and take a deep breath. Repeat this exercise until you feel the tension start to drain away. Remember, this exercise is to be done quietly so that no one knows you're relaxing!

DEALING WITH ANXIETY (Continued)

> **Andrew** is an accountant with a major financial organization. When he gives presentations he gets very nervous. He sweats, his hands tremble, his voice becomes a monotone (and at times inaudible). He also fidgets with items, such as a pen, and looks at his notes or the overhead projector screen, not at his audience. He can barely wait to finish and return to his seat.

Andrew's plight is not uncommon. You may not have all of these symptoms but you can probably relate to some of them. The following techniques will help you in situations where you get nervous while speaking.

7. *MOVE*

Speakers who stand in one spot and never gesture experience tension. In order to relax you need to release tension by allowing your muscles to flex. If you find you are locking your arms in one position when you speak, then practice releasing them so that they do the same thing they would if you were in an animated one-on-one conversation. You can't gesture too much if it is natural.

Upper body movement is important, but moving with your feet can serve to release tension as well. You should be able to take a few steps, either side-to-side or toward the audience. When speaking from a lectern you can move around the side of it for emphasis (if you have a moveable microphone). This movement will help release your tension and never fail to draw the audience into the presentation. If you can't move to the side of the lectern, an occasional half-step to one side will help loosen muscle tension.

8. *EYE CONTACT WITH THE AUDIENCE*

Try to make your presentation similar to a one-on-one conversation. Relate with your audience as individuals. Look in peoples' eyes as you speak. Connect with them. Make it personal and personable. The eye contact should help you relax because you become less isolated from the audience, and learn to react to their interest in you.

SECTION REVIEW—DEALING WITH ANXIETY CHECKLIST

Check those items which you intend to practice and incorporate in the future presentations you make.

I plan to:

☐ Organize my material

☐ Visualize myself delivering a successful presentation

☐ Rehearse by standing up and using all of my visual aids

☐ Breathe deeply just prior to speaking

☐ Focus on relaxing with simple, unobtrusive isometric techniques

☐ Release my tension in a positive way by directing it to my audience

☐ Move when I speak to stay relaxed and natural

☐ Maintain good eye contact with my audience

PRACTICE MAKES PERFECT

SECTION III: PLANNING THE PRESENTATION

Part of planning a presentation means that you must ask yourself why, not what. The "what" part will be answered when you begin to organize your thoughts. In the beginning you should concern yourself with *why* you are giving a presentation to a particular audience. The answer to this question should help you plan your presentation.

For example, you have been asked to give a presentation to a group of managers in your company on next year's departmental budget. Don't start writing down what you expect to say. Instead, ask yourself what you want to accomplish with your presentation. Will you be asking for a budget increase, or presenting a plan showing how you can operate on less money? Think about your specific objectives in relation to your audience before preparing your presentation.

PLANNING YOUR PRESENTATION

Can you imagine building a house without a set of plans? Before anyone can build a house, they need plans to guide the purchase of their materials and to show how these materials will be used. In the same way, a plan for your presentation will make the actual work of putting it together much more efficient. A two-step process—developing objectives and analyzing your audience—will help.

STEP #1 - Develop Objectives

The first step is to write down in a simple sentence what your objective(s) might be. For example: ''My objective is to inform my audience about progress on my research,'' or, ''My objective is to persuade upper management to grant my department a 20% budget increase.'' Business and technical presentations generally are either informative or persuasive. The difference between the two is explained below.

In an informative presentation you normally are not trying to change anyone's behavior, attitude, or beliefs. You are simply delivering the facts. An example of this type of presentation would be a report in which you simply inform others about progress on a project.

In a persuasive presentation you are trying to change some aspects of your audience's behavior, attitude or beliefs. For example you may want them to buy into your plans; give you money; change directions on the project; etc. The majority of presentations delivered in professional settings are persuasive.

PLANNING YOUR PRESENTATION (Continued)

STEP #2 - Analyzing Your Audience

Put yourself in the shoes of the people who will be listening to your presentation!

When analyzing your audience you have three items to consider:

1. **What are the values, needs and constraints on your audience?**
   With smaller groups you can provide more in-depth analysis because you usually know more about the individuals that comprise that group. In larger groups you may have to look at more general concepts.

2. **What is the knowledge level of the audience?**
   Have you ever been in a situation where the presenter used abbreviations, acronyms or technical terms that were unfamiliar to the audience? If you have any doubts, it is best to assume that the audience does not understand any specialized terms you might use. If some must be used, following your introduction, briefly explain those terms in simple language.

3. **What will work, what won't work?**
   You need to ask yourself what types of arguments and evidence will gain the most favorable reaction from the audience. And conversely, what types of arguments and evidence will gain an unfavorable reaction. Then plan your remarks accordingly.

PLANNING YOUR PRESENTATION (Continued)

This form should help you plan more efficiently for any presentation.

AUDIENCE ANALYSIS WORKSHEET

1. My objectives in relation to my audience are:

    _____

    _____

2. Values that need to be considered with this particular audience include:

    _____

    _____

3. Special needs of this particular audience:

    _____

    _____

4. Constraints that must be recognized when speaking to this particular audience.

    _____

    _____

5. I would rate my audience's knowledge of the topic and technical terminology to be:

    High _____   Low _____   Mixed _____   Unknown _____

6. My assessment of the audience's willingness to accept the ideas I present is:

    High _____   Low _____   Mixed _____   Unknown _____

7. My audience has an opinion of me as a speaker prior to the presentation of:

    Good _____   Poor _____   Mixed _____   Unknown _____

8. Examples of supporting ideas and arguments likely to work well:

    _____

    _____

9. Examples of supporting ideas and arguments are likely to cause a negative reaction_____

    _____

*This sheet may be reproduced without additional permission of the publisher.

SECTION IV: ORGANIZING YOUR PRESENTATION

This section will provide several steps which will assist you in organizing your thoughts for all future presentations. You will probably want to refer to this section of *Effective Presentation Skills* prior to your next several speaking assignments.

ORGANIZING YOUR THOUGHTS

It is always a good idea to start organizing the body of the speech and not worry about the introduction until later. Introductions are often generated by what goes into the body. Effective speakers have learned to build from the center of their speech outward. Following are some suggestions that might help you:

STEP #1 - Brainstorm Main Ideas

Using 3x5 index cards or Post-It Notes*, brainstorm some possible main ideas for your presentation. Write one idea on each card. Let the ideas flow at this point, don't edit, (that will come later). The strategy is to generate as many ideas as possible.

Once you have a large number of ideas, begin eliminating some. Try to end up with between two and five main ideas. This is a typical number for a presentation. If you have more than five ideas you should reduce them by making some of them subpoints.

EXAMPLE

Suppose you were asked to give a presentation to upper management to defend the need for your department's request for a 20% budget increase next year. You know it is going to be a persuasive presentation, and you have completed your audience analysis sheet (page 15). You created 10 to 15 original ideas to focus on and have narrowed them down to the following three:

| We need to update our computer system | More programmers are needed to develop our systems | We must finance development |

These three ideas are the general assertions you plan to make to your audience. Specific explanations, evidence and benefits will become your subpoints.

---

*Post-It is a registered trade mark of the 3M Company.

ORGANIZING YOUR THOUGHTS (Continued)

STEP #2 - State the Subpoints

Once you have the main points of your presentation, it is time to develop supporting ideas. These may consist of explanations, data or other evidence to support your main ideas as shown in our example.

			Main Ideas (General Assentions)
We need to update our computer system	More programmers are needed to develop our systems	We must finance development	

			Sub Ideas (Specifics)
Old system is antiquated	Will save $ immediately by creating proprietary programs	Need new data communications system	
Can't use latest software	Will be less dependent on outside vendors	New technology allows for better quality at same cost	
Old system costs are increasing because of inefficency	Can reassign most from within company	New personnel will contribute fresh ideas	
Many breakdowns recently	Will help keep us competitive	Need new programs	
Hard to replace parts	Can develop new products	New high speed printers will help develop new products	

You may have more or less subpoints in your presentation. Once you have completed this procedure, rearrange your cards to best suit your needs. Try different arrangements to see what will work best. Always keep your objectives and audience in mind.

ORGANIZING YOUR THOUGHTS (Continued)

STEP #3 - State the Benefits

In persuasive presentations it is necessary to tell the audience *specifically* what benefits they will receive if they do what you ask. Benefits can be stated before going into the body of your presentation, or at the end of the body, or ideally, in both places. From the previous example (Why our department needs a 20% larger budget next year) we might summarize the following benefits to our audience:

1. More money in our department will allow for a new computer system that will keep us competitive in our industry.

2. It, along with the necessary programmers, will increase profits because of greater efficiency.

3. A new system will allow us to upgrade our existing products, as well as develop new ones.

STEP #4 - Develop Handouts

Now you can decide what handouts (if any) would add to your presentation. Following are three major uses of handouts in a presentation:

1. To reinforce important information.

2. To summarize action items for the audience to follow up on.

3. To supply supporting data you don't want cluttering your visual aids.

ORGANIZING YOUR THOUGHTS (Continued)

STEP #4 - Developing Handouts (Continued)

Once you have decided what handouts would be beneficial you must then decide when you are going to hand them out. There are three alternatives:

BEFORE THE PRESENTATION

The main problem with this is that your audience may wish to satisfy their curiosity about the contents of your handout as you are speaking. When people are reading, they are not listening. One way to deal with this problem is to have the handout in place when the audience enters the room. This will allow them to read it before you begin speaking. In addition, you can explain the handout, satisfying their curiosity about its contents.

DURING THE PRESENTATION

This must be used carefully. Handouts during a presentation must be disbursed quickly and be relevant to the point you are making. Otherwise they will be a distraction, not an aid.

AT THE END OF THE PRESENTATION

During your presentation you can inform the audience that they will receive a handout covering such-and such points at the end of your presentation. This will allow them to not take unnecessary notes.

STEP #5 - Develop Visual Aids

Once your organizational pattern has been established, you need to decide if and where you are going to use visual aids. Guidelines for developing and using visuals in a presentation are discussed later (beginning on page 25). For now it is important only that you determine how they will fit into your plan.

For example, the third subpoint under the first major idea in our sample presentation developed on page 18, states that the old computer system is costing the company money. This point could be illustrated with a graph, or similar visual, showing the cost of the computer over the past three years versus the savings of a new system during the same time span.

ORGANIZING YOUR THOUGHTS (Continued)

Have you ever heard the saying:

Tell them what you're going to tell them—
Tell them—
Then tell them what you told them!

In other words, preview and review the main points in your presentation. This can be accomplished very easily by using a main idea preview sentence and a main idea review sentence. These sentences are separate from the introduction and conclusion.

Going back to the three main points in our example which were:

We need to update our computer	More programmers are needed to develop our systems	We must finance development

(Remember our objective is to convince upper management that our department needs a 20% larger budget for the next fiscal year.) The main idea preview sentence then is, *"We need to update our computer system, hire more programmers and finance development for several reasons which I will share with you today."* Before the conclusion you can use a similar sentence to review the main ideas as well; (i.e. *"You have now seen why an updated computer system, adequate staff and budget for new development is a good idea."*)

All effective presentations make the pattern of organization crystal clear to the audience.

ORGANIZING YOUR THOUGHTS (Continued)

STEP #7 - Develop the Introduction

You are now ready to develop your introduction. Introductions can serve a number of important purposes. These include:

1. To get the audience's attention and make them focus on you, the speaker.

2. To provide background information on your topic.

3. To introduce yourself—tell them who you are and why you are qualified to speak on the topic.

Regardless of the purpose, a good introduction is essential. There are various devices that you can use in an introduction, in addition to providing background material to help get the audience's attention. Here are some of the best:

Anecdote—

An anecdote is a short story used to help illustrate a point. It is sometimes humorous but not always. An example might be something like this. *"My son came to me the other day and said, 'Dad, if you raise my allowance by $2.00 I'll double mow the lawn each week. For another 10% you will get the best looking lawn in the neighborhood.' In the same way, if we raise salaries for our production workers 10%, we should expect to increase productivity."*

Humor—

Humor is a great way to break the ice. But beware! Humor must be linked to either the speaker, topic, audience or the occasion.

There is nothing worse than a joke used in an introduction that has no connection to the speech (i.e. *"Did you hear about the duck who walked into the store, ordered a lot of items and asked it all to be put on his bill? Well, today I would like to talk about data processing in our organization."*). Nothing is more embarrassing than a joke that falls flat.

ORGANIZING YOUR THOUGHTS (Continued)

STEP #7 - Develop the Introduction (Continued)

Rhetorical Question—

A rhetorical question is a question with an obvious answer. An example is, *''How many people here want to make more money?''* This device is an excellent way to get the audience's attention.

Shocking Statement—

A statement such as, *''Last year enough people died in automobile accidents to fill every seat in the local university's football stadium. This is why I am going to convince you to wear seatbelts.''* This type of statement will help capture your audience's attention.

STEP #8 - Develop the Conclusion

Good conclusions always return to material in your introduction. They normally should reference the background material, rhetorical question, anecdote or data that you used in your introduction.

In persuasive presentations you sometimes need a ''call-to-action'' statement in your conclusion. Tell your audience what they need to do (i.e. should they call a section meeting to implement that new solution? Should they give you that budget increase?) Your conclusion should tell them what specific action they need to take, how to take it, and when it must be taken.

Introductions and conclusions put the head and tail on the body of your presentation. Without them, or with them not fully developed, you don't have a complete presentation and it will be evident to the audience.

PLANNING AND ORGANIZING YOUR PRESENTATION REVIEW CHECKLIST

(Use this sheet to help prepare your next presentation)

Plan Your Presentation:

For my presentation I have:

- ☐ Developed Objectives
- ☐ Analyzed the Audience

Organize Your Presentation:

For this presentation I have:

- ☐ Brainstormed Main Ideas
- ☐ Brainstormed Sub Ideas
- ☐ Planned Handouts
- ☐ Planned Visual Aids
- ☐ Stated the Benefits (in persuasive presentations)
- ☐ Stated the Main Idea Preview/Review Sentence
- ☐ Structured the Introduction
- ☐ Developed the Conclusion

SECTION V: DEVELOPING AND USING VISUAL AIDS

In this section you will learn how to prepare and use visual aids in your speech. Most presentations in the business and professional world use overhead transparencies, so we will focus on their use. However, tips on using flipcharts, 35mm slides and other media are also covered in this section.

USE VISUAL AIDS WHEN YOU NEED TO:

1. Focus the audience's attention.

2. Reinforce your verbal message (but not repeat it verbatim!).

3. Stimulate interest.

4. Illustrate factors that are hard to visualize.

DON'T USE VISUAL AIDS TO:

1. Impress your audience with overly detailed tables or graphs.

2. Avoid interaction with your audience.

3. Make more than one main point.

4. Present simple ideas that are easily stated verbally.

DEVELOPING AND USING VISUAL AIDS
(Continued)

When constructing visual aids employ the K.I.S.S. principle—keep it short and simple! Don't overload charts with too much data. When you do, your audience will quickly lose interest, or get lost.

Avoid charts like this one.

Table of Monthly Social Security Benefits

Average Indexed Monthly Earnings (AIME)	Benefits For Living Workers And Their Dependents						Benefits For Survivors of Deceased Workers					Maximum Family Benefit for Survivors and Retirement
	Age 65 Retirement Benefit or Disability Benefit (2)	Age 62 Retirement Benefit	Benefits for Dependents		Child or Spouse Caring for Child	Maximum Family Benefit for Disability	Spouse Not Caring for Child		One Child Alone	One Parent	Spouse and One Child or Two Children Alone or Two Parents	
			Spouse Not Caring for Child (3)				Age 65 (4) (5)	Age 60 or Age 50-59 & Disabled				
			Age 65	Age 62								
400	282	226	141	106	141	340(6)	282	202	212	233	424	424
450	298	239	149	112	149	382(6)	298	213	224	246	448	448
500	314	251	157	118	157	425(6)	314	225	236		472	472
550	330	264	165	124	165	467(6)	330	236				496
600	346	277	173	130	173	510(6)	346	247				526
650	362	290	181	136	181	544	362	259				569
700	378	303	189	142	189	568	378	270				613
750	394	315	197	148	197	592	394	282				656
800	410	328	205	154	205	616	410	297				700
850	426	341	213	160	213	640	426	30				743
900	442	354	221	166	221	664	442	316				787
950	458	367	229	172	229	688	458	328				830
1,000	474	379	237	178	237	712	474	339				874
1,100	506	405	253	190	253	760	506	362				942
1,200	538	431	269	202	269	808	538	385				985
1,300	570	456	285	214	285	856	570	408	428			1,027
1,400	602	482	301	226	301	904	602	431	452	497	904	1,070
1,500	634	507	317	238	317	952	634	453	476	523	952	1,113
1,600	666	533	333	250	333	1,000	666	476	500	550	1,000	1,166
1,700	683	547	341	256	341	1,025	683	488	512	564	1,025	1,196
1,800(7)	698	559	249	262	349	1,048	698	499	524	576	1,048	1,222
1,900	713	571	356	267	356	1,070	713	510	535	588	1,070	1,248
2,000	728	583	364	273	364	1,093	728	521	546	601	1,093	1,275
2,100	743	595	371	278	371	1,115	743	531	557	613	1,115	1,301
2,200	758	607	379	284	379	1,138	758	542	569	626	1,138	1,327
2,300	773	619	386	290	286	1,160	773	553	580	683	1,160	1,353
2,400	788	631	394	295	394	1,183	788	564	591	650	1,183	1,380
2,500	803	643	401	301	401	1,205	803	574	602	663	1,205	1,406
2,600	818	655	409	307	409	1,228	818	585	614	675	1,228	1,432
2,700	833	667	416	312	416	1,250	833	596	625	687	1,250	1,458
2,800(8)	848	679	424	318	424	1,273	848	606	636	700	1,273	1,485
2,900	863	691	431	323	431	1,295	863	617	647	712	1,295	1,511
3,000(9)	878	703	439	329	439	1,318	878	628	659	725	1,318	1,537

AVOID THIS

Simplify the chart and focus audience attention where you want it.

INFORMATION CONTENT GUIDELINES FOR NUMBER CHARTS

NUMBER CHARTS—**USE A MAXIMUM OF 30 NUMBERS PER VISUAL AID.**
One number can have up to 5 digits—for example, 18,922 counts as one number.
Going above this number of digits causes the visual to look too crowded, and the
focus becomes lost.

AVOID THIS

MONTHLY CUMULATIVE TOTALS

	Accepts	Volume	Returns	Amount
	179.880	423.3660	967	334.07
	128.864	345.7670	860	287.74
	34.221	678.4440	733	982.21
	129.775	654.9980	1887	658.89
	378.664	739.6000	431	295.58
	194.775	187.4659	223	295.50
	198.856	189.9570	582	377.89
	746.599	879.9560	334	867.73
	286.675	385.7689	233	286.57
	196.999	285.8678	188	296.97
	185.868	286.8786	299	185.90
Totals:	2661.767	5058.3140	6737	4869.13

In this case, *only the totals line* is essential—the rest of the information *could be put in a handout.*

THIS IS BETTER

MONTHLY CUMULATIVE TOTALS

Accepts	Volume	Returns	Amount
2661	5058	6737	4869

Avoid "Data Dump". Crowding your presentation with too many visuals and/or too much information will reduce their effectiveness and you will lose impact. Usually the fewer, the better!

INFORMATION CONTENT GUIDELINES FOR WORD CHARTS

FOR WORD CHARTS—**USE A MAXIMUM OF 36 WORDS PER VISUAL AID** (excluding the title). Try to fit your material into a maximum of six lines, with no more than six words per line. If you need more room, (as in the example below), use more lines, but fewer words. There is no need to repeat every word in your presentation. You simply want to reinforce your main ideas to the audience.

HOW TO ORGANIZE YOUR PRESENTATION

It is a good idea to start by developing objectives. Once this is done you need to thoroughly analyze the audience. You must complete these steps before you separately brainstorm the main points and the subpoints of your presentation. If it's a persuasive presentation, then you also must decide what the benefits are. You then gather factual information and prepare a blueprint of your presentation. Also prepare any visual aids, handouts and notes you will need. And don't forget to practice!

AVOID THIS

This chart is more effective when it is set up as follows:

HOW TO ORGANIZE YOUR PRESENTATION

1. Develop Objectives

2. Analyze the Audience

3. Brainstorm the Main Ideas and the Sub Ideas

4. Develop Visuals, Handouts and Notes

5. State the Benefits (in a persuasive presentation)

6. State Main Idea Preview/Review Sentence

7. Structure Introduction and Conclusion

THIS IS BETTER

Stating information clearly and concisely on your charts makes it easier for the audience to retain information.

Following are several examples of how different types of information can be effectively presented using visual aids.

CHART AND GRAPH SELECTION–TYPES OF CHARTS

PERCENT–Shows a comparison as a percentage of the whole. Usually uses the pie chart or map chart.

COMPANY EXPENDITURES

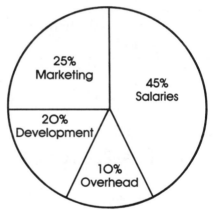

PARTS–Shows how items compare or rank. Usually a bar (horizontal lines) or column chart (vertical lines).

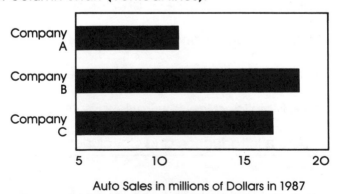

Auto Sales in millions of Dollars in 1987

CHART AND GRAPH SELECTION—TYPES OF CHARTS (Continued)

TIME–Shows changes over a period of time. Column or line charts are most typical.

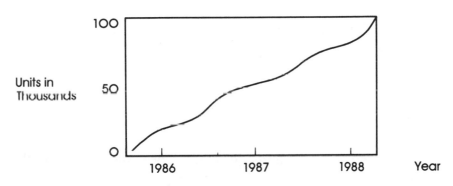

FREQUENCY–Shows the number of items in different numerical ranges. Column and line charts are also used here.

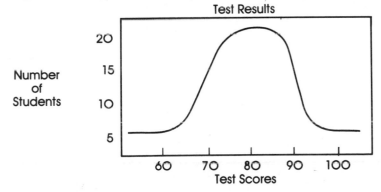

CORRELATION–Shows the relationship between variables. Bar charts and dot charts are used to illustrate correlation.

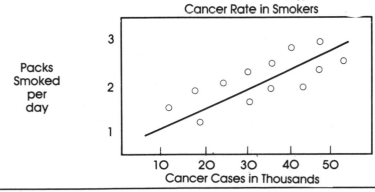

DEVELOPING VISUAL AIDS (Continued)

Developing Titles for your Visual Aids

There are three basic types of titles for your visual aids. Choose the one that best suits your needs:

Topic Title—Used when it is not necessary to convey a specific message but only provide information or raw data, as in the example below:

Sales Figures

Thematic Title—Used to tell the audience what information they should draw from the data presented. An example would be:

Sales in 1987 were up 22% over 1986

Assertive Title—Used when you want to give the audience your opinion about what conclusion they should draw from the data. It is used most often in persuasive presentations, as in the following example:

We should focus our sales effort in the Western U.S.

HINT:

Make your presentation one that is people-centered, not media-centered. Too many presentations rely on the media to carry the message. While the media can certainly help, it's your interaction and rapport with the audience that makes the difference between an effective or ineffective presentation.

USING VISUAL AIDS IN YOUR PRESENTATION

Case Study

Jack has to give a presentation to his engineering group outlining a major new project he is proposing for the company. He has spent weeks preparing for this 30 minute presentation. This project is important to Jack, and he is very nervous about presenting it.

Jack prepared 75 overhead transparencies for the presentation. Each is crammed with information. As the presentation begins Jack finds that he is spending more time than he thought he would discussing each transparency. His allotted time is going to by very quickly. He speeds up his rate of speech, and to finish on time he shows the last 35 transparencies without any discussion.

Case Study

Gene works in a large bank. He must make a presentation on the past, present and future of the bank's corporate finance department to a group of high-ranking department managers. Gene is very anxious to have his presentation go well.

In Gene's 30 minute presentation he will use overhead transparencies, and he has prepared 10 that summarize important information from his written report. Each transparency deals with a single issue, yet has enough information to cover the subject and reinforce the points Gene is trying to make. He knows that a summary of information on his visual aids will provide enough meat for discussion. Gene's philosophy is to make the visual aids work for him, and not let them overwhelm the presentation.

Who do you think was more successful, and why?

_____

_____

_____

_____

USING VISUAL AIDS IN YOUR PRESENTATION
(Continued)

Directing your audience's focus

Learn to direct the audience's focus where you want it. When you use visual aids, the audience's focus is divided. To "win them back" you will need to redirect their focus. This is usually done by closing down the visuals, and taking a step or two towards the audience.

> Place a check next to the technique(s) that you plan to use in the presentation you give.

I plan to:

_____ Shut off the overhead projector when there is a lengthy explanation about a point in the transparency and there is no need for the audience to watch the screen. I won't click the machine on and off in a distracting way, but also won't leave it on so long that they focus on the transparency and not on me.

_____ Turn a flip-chart page when I have finished referring to it. If the flip charts have been prepared in advance, I plan to leave three blank pages between each prepared sheet so my next page won't show until I'm ready for it.

_____ Erase any writing I have on a blackboard for the reasons outlined above. Any information noted by the audience and no longer needed for future reference can be erased.

_____ Break up slide presentations by inserting a black slide at points where an explanation is needed, or when I want to make a transition to another section. This will wake up my audience and help refocus their attention. I will leave some light on in the room, near where I am standing so that I become the focus of attention when the screen goes black.

USING VISUAL AIDS IN YOUR PRESENTATION
(Continued)

_____ Show or demonstrate an object by revealing it when it is referred to and then covering it up when it is no longer in use. If the object is not covered, most people will continue looking out of curiosity and may miss some of my presentation.

_____ Avoid passing objects around the audience since this is very distracting. Instead, I will walk into the audience and show the object to everyone briefly and, then, make it available at the end of the session.

> Decide in advance where the audience should focus. Do you want the focus divided between you and the visual aid or do you need their undivided attention?

USING VISUAL AIDS IN YOUR PRESENTATION (Continued)

Placement of Equipment

When using an overhead projector or flipchart, you should add, not detract, from your presentation. This can be accomplished by placing the overhead screen or flipchart at a 45 degree angle and slightly to one side of the center of the room. In this way a presenter can occupy the central position and more easily focus the audience's attention on the explanation of the data being displayed.

Figure #1 shows how a room can be set up to maximize audience focus on the speaker. Figure #2 shows the room set up where the speaker is competing for attention with the visuals.

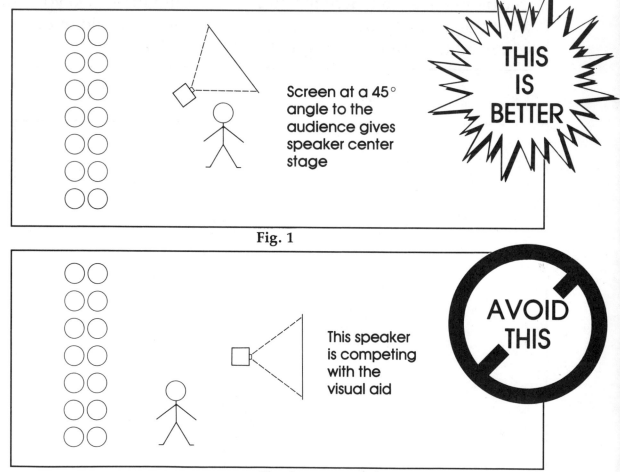

Fig. 1

Fig. 2

USING VISUAL AIDS IN YOUR PRESENTATION (Continued)

Where and How to Stand

One major problem when using visual aids is that speakers often give their presentation to the visuals, and not to the audience. This problem can be easily corrected if the speaker remembers to keep shoulder orientation toward the audience at all times as illustrated in figure #1. Figure #2 shows what happens when your shoulders turn toward the visuals.

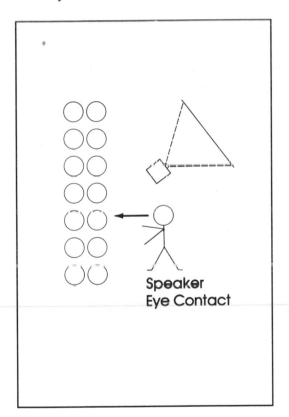

Fig. 1

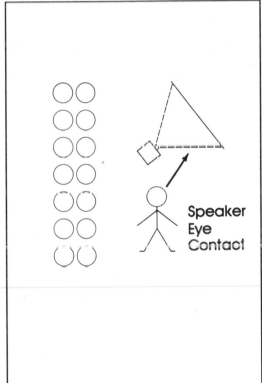

Fig. 2

Remember: Don't speak until you have eye contact with your audience! If you must write something on the flipchart, overhead or white board, stop talking while you write.

USING VISUAL AIDS IN YOUR PRESENTATION (Continued)

Tips on using a pointer:

1. Pointers should be used to make a *quick* visual reference on a pictorial chart or to trace the relationship of data on a graph. Pointers are not needed on word charts since you can refer to each point by an item or number.

2. When using a pointer, keep your shoulder oriented toward the audience. Do not cross your arm over your body to refer to something on the screen. Instead, hold the pointer in the hand closest to the screen.

3. Don't play with the pointer when not using it. Either fold it up and put it away, or put it down.

4. Use your pointer at the screen, not the overhead projector. Standing at the projector will often block somebody's view of the screen.

5. Leaving the pointer on the overhead projector can focus too much attention on the screen and could detract from the speaker.

SECTION REVIEW: DEVELOPING AND USING VISUALS AIDS

> Check those items you plan to incorporate in your presentation.

I expect to:

☐ Use the KISS* principle when designing visuals and not overload my audience.

☐ Use "key words" or phrases only for my word charts.

☐ Talk to my audience, not to my visual aids.

☐ Place myself at center stage.

☐ Use pointers sparingly and not nervously fiddle with them.

---

*Keep It Simple Sweetheart

SECTION VI: PREPARING FOR YOUR PRESENTATION

In preparing for your presentation you must practice and rehearse as much as possible. This will help you do the very best job you can.

Sometimes a presentation must be prepared at the last minute, leaving little time for preparation and practice. This situation usually leads to increased anxiety on the part of the speaker and often to a less than professional presentation. Later in this book there are some techniques for organizing impromptu or ''on-the-spot'' presentations.

THIS IS MR. FOGARTY. HE'S DROPPED BY WITH A FEW OF HIS ACCOUNTANTS AND ATTORNEYS. GIVE HIM A REVIEW OF HIS ACCOUNT, WILL YOU, MISS JOHNSON?

PREPARE FOR YOUR PRESENTATION

How To Practice Your Presentation

Following is a checklist for your practice sessions. Staying aware of these steps will help you give a more relaxed, confident and enthusiastic presentation.

_____ Make sure your notes are ''key words'' only, printed in large letters on index cards. This will provide you with recall cues without having you ''read'' to your audience.

_____ Mentally run through the presentation to review each idea in sequence.

_____ Repeat the above procedure until you become familiar with the flow of ideas and where you plan to use visual aids to support them.

_____ Begin stand-up rehearsals of your presentation. Try to arrange a practice room similar to the one in which you will actually give your presentation.

_____ Give a simulated presentation, idea-for-idea (not word-for-word), using all visual aids. Use minimum focus on the notes, maximum focus on the audience.

_____ Practice answers to questions you anticipate from the audience.

_____ Give the full presentation again. If possible, videotape yourself or have a friend give you some feedback.

_____ Review the videotape and/or the friend's feedback and incorporate any necessary changes.

_____ Give one or two dress rehearsals with the presentation in its final form.

CONTROLLING THE PRESENTATION ENVIRONMENT

> **Larry** worked all week preparing for his quarterly presentation. He has rehearsed (standing up and using his visual aids) and feels prepared and confident. The morning of his presentation he arrived early in order to go over his material one final time.
>
> As he enters the meeting room for his presentation he notices his manager and his department head in the audience. He is anxious but knows he is prepared. He begins his presentation and then moves to the overhead projector to show his first transparency. He flips the switch and nothing happens. He notices the unit is plugged in. He next checks the bulb only to find it's burned out. He knows that most overhead projectors have spare bulbs, but when he looks for it he realizes someone didn't bother to replace it. It takes him 20 minutes to track down a new bulb.

This situation could have been avoided if Larry had checked the projector in advance. A few minutes of planning, checking equipment and arranging seating can prevent disasters. Presenters can usually exercise a degree of control over their speaking environment. Following are eight items to think about before you speak:

1. Overhead Projectors

Make sure that the bulb is not burned out and that there is a spare bulb available. Cleaning the projection screen can sharpen the image. Do you need clear sheets as write-on overlays and pens to use on them?

2. Flip Charts

Is there enough paper? Do you have a supply of marking pens available? Have you checked to insure they have not dried out?

3. Slide Projectors

Is it in working condition? Is the lens large enough to project the image size you need? Does your slide holder fit the projector? Is it located so the image will fit the screen? Does it have a remote switch that works, or can you recruit someone to operate it for you? Have you practiced using the machine?

CONTROLLING THE PRESENTATION ENVIRONMENT (Continued)

4. Handouts

Are handouts easily accessible and in order, so they can be handed out with minimum disruption? Have you arranged for assistance in handing them out if needed?

5. Pointers

Will you need a pointer? Is it easily accessible, so you can use it when you need it during the presentation?

6. Microphones

If speaking to more than 50-100 people you will probably need a microphone. Before your presentation you may want to request a microphone that allows you to move around. You can request a hand-held mike with a 10-15 foot extension cord or a lavelier mike that will hook on your jacket or tie and allow you to keep your hands free.

7. Lighting

Do you need to dim the lights in the room? Check to see if there is a dimmer switch. Having some light on in the room is desirable in 35mm slide presentations, so you won't be a voice in the dark. Check to see that all the bulbs and fixtures in the room are working.

8. Seating Arrangement

If you have control over seating in a room, exercise it. If possible arrange the seating so that the exit and entrance to the room are at the rear. In this way, if people come and go, it will cause the least amount of distraction.

If you know about how many people are going to be present try to control the seating so that there are approximately as many seats as people. This way you won't have your audience sitting in the back of the room. Keeping your audience closer will focus their attention where you want it.

WHEN YOU CAN'T PRACTICE YOUR PRESENTATION— SUCCESSFUL IMPROMPTU SPEAKING

> **Jill** is invited, along with her manager, to attend a meeting of all department heads in the company. She is not expecting to say anything, only to sit and listen. During her manager's presentation, he is asked a question about the department's plans for the coming year. He turns to Jill and says, ''Jill, you've been working on our major project for the past year. Maybe you could say a few words about how this project got started, where it stands and where it is going.''

If something like this happens to you, don't panic! You already know the fundamentals of organizing your thoughts, and you know your job. With these two resources you can effectively respond by taking the following steps:

Think:

Plug into a pattern of organization.
Any topic can be split up into components. Before you speak break your topic into a pattern such as:

  A) past, present and future (or any time-oriented combination),

  B) topic 1, 2 and 3 (e.g. production, advertising and marketing);

  C) the pro's and con's of an issue (useful in persuasive situations).

In Jill's case above, the time-ordered sequence fits right in.

Then speak:

Give a few introductory remarks.
Before you launch into the meat of your topic give yourself time to get collected. Make some general introductory comments, such as, ''Thanks, boss, I'm pleased to be here today to help provide some information. I didn't plan a formal presentation but would be happy to describe the project we've been working on.''

Develop a clear preview sentence of your main points.
You will want to verbalize to yourself and your audience what your key points are. From the example above Jill could simply state, ''I would like to tell you about how we started this project, where it stands and where we plan to take it''; which is a time ordered sequence.

SUCCESSFUL IMPROMPTU SPEAKING (Continued)

Deliver the body of the presentation.
Talk through each point from your preview sentence. (In Jill's example; past, present and future). Having an organizational pattern established and knowing where you are going will take some of the stress out of the situation.

If what you are speaking about is controversial, first acknowledge the opposition's case but finish with your viewpoint so you end by summarizing your position.

Review the main points.
Reinforce the main ideas you've touched upon by briefly restating them. Something like, "I've tried in these past few minutes to give you an overview of how this project started, where it is now and where we think it will go."

Conclude the presentation.
Don't leave your presentation high and dry. Conclude it with a strong, positive, statement. Following our example, "I hope to attend next month's meeting to report a satisfactory conclusion to our project. I would be happy to take any questions at this time."

SECTION REVIEW–PREPARE FOR YOUR PRESENTATION

1. Rehearse your presentation, standing up and using your visual aids.

2. Control the environment by checking:

   - seating arrangements

   - lighting

   - microphones

   - handouts

   - pointers

   - projection equipment to insure it is available, in working condition, and has the required back-up supplies

3. When you have to give an impromptu presentation:

   - plug into a pattern of organization

   - give a few introductory remarks

   - preview and review the main points for your audience

   - end with a strong conclusion

SECTION VII: DELIVERING THE PRESENTATION

You must communicate your enthusiasm to the audience if you want them to be enthusiastic about the ideas you present.

Standing stiffly, with little animation in your body, and speaking in a monotone voice without good eye contact is a sure way to deliver a speech that is a dud. We communicate with much more than words. Your nonverbal actions carry your feelings. If these channels get cut off because of anxiety, your interaction and rapport with the audience will suffer.

A great benefit of providing an interactive and animated presentation style is that your nervous energy will flow in a positive form and not stay in your body. Seek a natural, conversational style, relate to people in the audience in a direct and personable manner. Even in the most formal situations this is a necessity.

You must learn to be aware of not only what you are saying but also how you are saying it! Learn to be your own coach while you are up in front of the audience, checking the items outlined in this section.

DELIVERING THE PRESENTATION

Deliver Your Presentation in the Following Sequence

1. Introduction

2. Preview sentence (Tell them what you're going to tell them)

3. Main Ideas and Sub Ideas (Tell them)

4. Benefits (In persuasive presentations)

5. Review Sentence (Tell them what you told them)

6. Conclusion

DELIVERING THE PRESENTATION (Continued)

The following tips will help your presentation become animated, interesting and engaging. If you can videotape a rehearsal, watch your delivery. Then rehearse again using some of the techniques described below. Experiment with different presentation styles until you find one that is comfortable and effective.

POSTURE

Keep your posture erect but relaxed. You want to stand up straight but not stiff. Your feet should be pointed at the audience with your weight evenly distributed. Don't place your weight on one hip, then shift to the other and back again. This shifting can distract the audience.

MOVEMENT

Typically, speakers tend to stand in one spot, feet rooted like a tree to the ground. If your presentation will be delivered from a lectern, you should experiment. If appropriate, move to the side or front of the lectern to get nearer the audience. Many professional speakers do this. It is engaging, and audiences feel closer to the speaker without barriers. If you are using a microphone, then you will need an extension cord or lavelier mike. In a formal presentation, or if the lectern is at a head table, this technique may not be practical.

When not using a lectern, you should normally stay within 4-8 feet of the front row. Don't stay frozen in one spot but don't pace either. An occasional step to either side, or even a half-step towards the audience for emphasis, can enhance your presentation. Stay close, stay direct, and stay involved with your audience.

DELIVERING THE PRESENTATION (Continued)

GESTURES

The importance of natural gestures, uninhibited by anxiety, cannot be overstated. Too often anxiety holds back this important channel of communication. We use gestures for emphasis in normal conversation without thinking about what we are doing with our hands. *Learn to gesture in front of an audience exactly as you would if you were having an animated conversation with a friend—nothing more, nothing less.*

Using natural gestures won't distract from a presentation; however, doing one of the following certainly will:

Keeping hands in your pockets-

Or handcuffed behind your back-

Or keeping your arms crossed-

Or in a fig leaf position-

Or wringing your hands nervously-

DELIVERING THE PRESENTATION (Continued)

EYE CONTACT

Interviewing a person who looked at the wall or floor when answering your questions would not inspire your confidence in that person. In our culture we expect good, direct eye contact. Yet in many presentations, a speaker will look at a spot on the back of the wall, or at a screen, or at notes—everywhere but into the eyes of the audience.

Eye contact opens the channel of communication between people. It helps establish and build rapport. It involves the audience in the presentation, and makes the presentation more personable. (This is true even in formal presentations.) Good eye contact between the speaker and audience also helps relax the speaker by connecting the speaker to the audience and reducing the speaker's feeling of isolation.

The rule of thumb for eye contact is *1-3 seconds per person*. Try not to let your eyes dart around the room. Try to focus on one person, not long enough to make that individual feel uncomfortable, but long enough to pull him or her into your presentation. Then move on to another person.

When you give a presentation, don't just look at your audience—*see them*. Seek out individuals, and be aware that you are looking at them.

If the group is too large to look at each individual separately, make eye contact with individuals in different parts of the audience. People sitting near the individuals you select will feel that you are actually looking at them. As the distance between a speaker and audience increases, a larger and larger circle of people will feel your ''eye contact.''

DELIVERING THE PRESENTATION (Continued)

USING YOUR VOICE

There are three main problems associated with voice: a monotone, is an inappropriate rate of speech (usually talking too fast) or volume that is too loud or too soft. Make sure your voice is working for you. The following suggestions will help you speak with a strong, clear voice.

Monotone

Most monotone voices are caused by anxiety. As the speaker tightens up, the muscles in the chest and throat become less flexible and air flow is restricted. When this happens, the voice loses its natural animation and a monotone results.

To bring back the natural animation you must relax and release tension. Upper and lower body movement are vital. This doesn't have to be dramatic movement—just enough to loosen the muscles and get you to breathe normally. Videotaping, or audio taping, or feedback from a friend will let you know how you're doing.

> *Learn to listen to yourself; stay aware not only of what you are saying but also how you are saying it.*

Talking too fast.

Our average conversational rate of speech is about 125 words per minute. When we become anxious, that rate will usually increase. An increased rate of speech is not necessarily a problem if your articulation is good. However, if you are delivering a technical presentation, or one in which the audience needs to take notes, you need to watch your pace.

Another indication that you are talking too fast is when you trip over words. When this happens, slow down. Listen for yourself to say the last word of a sentence, pause where the period would be, and then proceed to your next sentence. Pausing during a presentation can be an effective device to allow your important points to sink in. Don't be afraid to allow periods of silence during your presentations. The audience needs time to digest what you are saying.

DELIVERING THE PRESENTATION (Continued)

Problems with volume.

In most cases, problems with volume can be solved with practice. You need to stay aware of your volume. It is appropriate to ask during an actual presentation, "Can you hear me in the back?" The audience will usually be honest because they want to hear what you are saying!

To find out if you have a volume problem before a presentation, ask someone who will give you a straight answer. Ask that person if you can be heard in the back of a room, if you trail off at the end of a sentence, if a lack of volume makes you sound insecure or if you are speaking too loudly.

If your problem is a soft voice, there is a simple exercise to learn how to increase your volume. Recruit two friends to help you. Go into a room that is at least twice the size of the one where you normally give presentations. Have one person sit in the front row, and the other stand against the back wall. Start speaking, and have the person in the back give you a signal when you can be heard clearly. Note your volume level. How does it feel? Check with the person in the front row to make sure you weren't too loud.

A voice consistently too loud sometimes indicates a slight hearing loss. If your voice is judged too loud you may wish to check with your doctor. If you check out OK, then do the above exercise again, but this time let the person in the front row give you a signal to soften your voice, and then check with the person in the back to make sure you can be heard.

QUESTION-AND-ANSWER TECHNIQUES

HOW TO ENCOURAGE YOUR AUDIENCE TO ASK QUESTIONS

Often you will want your audience to ask questions. When you have delivered technical information, complicated ideas or are leading a training session, it is a good idea to check audience comprehension by taking questions.

If you ask for questions passively you won't encourage a response. It's mostly a matter of body language. Standing away from the audience, hands stuffed in your pockets, and mumbling "Any questions?" does not encourage questions from an audience.

Those who actively seek questions will step toward the audience, raise a hand and ask, "Does anyone have questions for me?" You might also ask, "What questions do you have?" You *assume* the audience will ask questions, and they often do. Also, pause long enough after asking for questions, so the audience will have time to think of questions (the silence should get to them before it gets to you!) Raising your hand will accomplish two things. One, it is the visual signal for questions and will encourage those who might be shy. Also, it helps keep order. The audience will follow your lead and raise their hands, instead of yelling out their questions.

HOW TO LISTEN TO QUESTIONS

Perhaps you have seen a speaker listen to a question while pacing back and forth, not look at the question asker, and then interrupt with something like, "You don't have to finish, I know what you're asking." The speaker may not know what is being asked until the question is finished. It is important to wait until the questioner has finished.

While the question is being asked you should watch the person who is asking it. Often it is possible to pick up clues to the intensity of the question, the feelings behind it and any hidden agendas, if you are aware of body language.

During questions, be careful what you do with your hands! Imagine giving a presentation enthusiastically, and presenting your ideas confidently. Then imagine that when you receive a question, you stand looking at the floor rubbing your hands together nervously. This behavior can negate the confident image you provided during the presentation. Your hands should stay in a neutral position, arms at your sides, fingers open. Focus on the question and listen carefully.

QUESTION-AND-ANSWER TECHNIQUES
(Continued)

HOW TO ANSWER QUESTIONS

Prepare for questions. You should be able to anticipate most of the questions you receive. Practice answering them. Prepare for the worst and everything else will seem easier. Some speakers prepare back-up visual aids, just to be used when answering anticipated questions.

Repeat the question. If there is any chance that anyone in the audience didn't hear a question, repeat it for the whole audience. Or, if you get a complicated, emotional or multi-part question, restate it to make sure you understand it. Since we think approximately five times faster than we speak, repeating the question may give you a few extra seconds to formulate a good answer, too.

Maintain your style. When answering questions, it is important to maintain the same style and demeanor you used in the presentation. A change in demeanor can suggest that you are not confident about your position. When you're asked a question you don't know the answer to, you don't have to say, ''Sorry, I don't know the answer to that.'' Instead you can say, ''I don't know, but I'll find out and get back to you later.''

Involve the whole audience in your answer. Have you seen speakers who get involved with the person who has asked a question and ignore the rest of the audience? In some situations the questioner may try to ''hook'' the speaker with a difficult question. You can always tell if a speaker is ''hooked'' because he or she focuses only on the person who asked the question.

QUESTION-AND-ANSWER TECHNIQUES
(Continued)

Employ the 25%-75% rule. Direct approximately 25% of your eye contact to the person who asked the question and approximately 75% to the rest of the audience. (This is especially important in a hostile question and answer situation). Don't ignore the person who asked the question, but don't ignore the rest of the audience either. This will help you stay in command of the situation and keep the audience involved in your presentation.

Don't preface your answer. Sometimes, when we hear a speaker start an answer with, ''That's a very good question; I'm glad you asked it,'' it may be a sign that the speaker is unsure of the answer.

It's best not to preface answers but simply to go into the answer (after repeating the question, if appropriate). At the end of your question-and-answer session you can say something like, ''Thank you for all your excellent questions.''

Most presentations include time for questions and answers. Sometimes questions are asked during the session and, sometimes, at the end. In many cases a speaker has the option of where he or she would like to have questions asked. If this is the case, then you can ask the audience to interrupt you whenever they have questions, or you can request that they save their questions until you've finished the presentation.

SECTION REVIEW

DELIVERING YOUR PRESENTATION

I plan to:

☐ Stay aware of not only what is said, but how I say it.

☐ Be animated, enthusiastic and direct in my delivery.

☐ Use eye contact to make my presentation personable and conversational.

☐ Keep a clear, strong voice and not speak too fast.

QUESTION-AND-ANSWER TECHNIQUES

I plan to:

☐ Ask for questions by stepping forward with my hand raised.

☐ Anticipate questions and practice the answers.

☐ Watch the questioner and listen carefully to the question.

☐ Keep my hands in a neutral position when listening to questions.

☐ Repeat the question to make sure everyone heard it, or for clarification.

☐ Keep the same style and demeanor that I had during the presentation.

☐ Use eye contact and involve the whole audience in my answer.

EFFECTIVE PRESENTATIONS— QUICK REFERENCE CHECK LIST

Check the following items as you prepare and then deliver your presentation.

TO DEAL WITH ANXIETY—I PLAN TO:

☐ Breathe Deeply

☐ Focus on Relaxing

☐ Release Tension by Unobtrusive Isometrics

☐ Move During the Presentation

☐ Maintain Good Eye Contact with the Audience

TO PLAN AND ORGANIZE YOUR PRESENTATION—I WILL:

☐ Develop Objectives

☐ Analyze my Audience

☐ Brainstorm Main Ideas

☐ Brainstorm Sub Ideas

☐ Plan Handouts

☐ Plan Visual Aids

☐ State the Benefits

☐ Incorporate a Main Idea, Preview, and Review Sentence

☐ Structure my Introduction

☐ Develop a Strong Conclusion

EFFECTIVE PRESENTATIONS—
QUICK REFERENCE CHECK LIST (Continued)

TO DEVELOP AND USE VISUAL AIDS, I EXPECT TO:

☐ Use the KISS Principal

☐ Choose the Correct Type of Chart

☐ Use Appropriate Titles

☐ Refrain from Talking to the Visual Aids

☐ Place myslef at Center Stage

☐ Use my Pointer Sparingly

TO PREPARE FOR THE PRESENTATION, I WILL:

☐ Rehearse standing up and using visuals.

☐ Check seating, the AV equipment, all handouts, etc.

WHILE DELIVERING MY PRESENTATION, I PLAN TO:

☐ Stay aware of what I'm saying and how I say it.

☐ Be animated, enthusiastic and direct.

☐ Make my presentation personable and conversational.

☐ Use a clear, strong voice.

FOR QUESTION-AND-ANSWER SESSIONS, I PLAN TO:

☐ Raise my hand and step towards the audience.

☐ Watch and listen to the questioner.

☐ Repeat the question if necessary.

☐ Maintain my style and demeanor.

☐ Answer to the whole audience with my eye contact.

ABOUT THE FIFTY-MINUTE SERIES

"Fifty-Minute books are the best new publishing idea in years. They are clear, practical, concise and affordable — perfect for today's world."

Leo Hauser
(Past President, ASTD)

What Is A Fifty-Minute Book?

—Fifty-Minute books are brief, soft-cover, "self-study" modules which cover a single concept. They are reasonably priced, and ideal for formal training programs, excellent for self-study and perfect for remote location training.

Why Are Fifty-Minute Books Unique?

—Because of their format and level. Designed to be "read with a pencil," the basics of a subject can be quickly grasped and applied through a series of hands-on activities, exercises and cases.

How Many Fifty-Minute Books Are There?

—Those listed on the facing page at this time, however, additional titles are in development. For more information write to **Crisp Publications, Inc., 95 First Street, Los Altos, CA 94022.**

Crisp books are distributed in Canada by Reid Publishing, Ltd., P.O. Box 7267, Oakville, Ontario, Canada L6J 6L6.

In Australia by Prime Learning Australia, Rochedale South, 7 Deputor Street, Brisbane, Queensland.

And in New Zealand by Prime Learning Pacific, 18 Gibbons Road, Weymouth, Auckland.

THE FIFTY-MINUTE SERIES

Quantity	Title	Code #	Price	Amount
	The Fifty-Minute Supervisor—*2nd Edition*	58-0	$6.95	
	Effective Performance Appraisals—*Revised*	11-4	$6.95	
	Successful Negotiation—*Revised*	09-2	$6.95	
	Quality Interviewing—*Revised*	13-0	$6.95	
	Team Building: An Exercise in Leadership—*Revised*	16-5	$6.95	
	Performance Contracts: The Key To Job Success—*Revised*	12-2	$6.95	
	Personal Time Management	22-X	$6.95	
	Effective Presentation Skills	24-6	$6.95	
	Better Business Writing	25-4	$6.95	
	Quality Customer Service	17-3	$6.95	
	Telephone Courtesy & Customer Service	18-1	$6.95	
	Restaurant Server's Guide To Quality Service—*Revised*	08-4	$6.95	
	Sales Training Basics—*Revised*	02-5	$6.95	
	Personal Counseling—*Revised*	14-9	$6.95	
	Balancing Home & Career	10-6	$6.95	
	Mental Fitness: A Guide To Emotional Health	15-7	$6.95	
	Attitude: Your Most Priceless Possession	21-1	$6.95	
	Preventing Job Burnout	23-8	$6.95	
	Successful Self-Management	26-2	$6.95	
	Personal Financial Fitness	20-3	$7.95	
	Job Performance and Chemical Dependency	27-0	$7.95	
	Career Discovery *Revised*	07-6	$6.95	
	Study Skills Strategies—*Revised*	05-X	$6.95	
	I Got The Job!—*Revised*	59-9	$6.95	
	Effective Meetings Skills	33-5	$7.95	
	The Business of Listening	34-3	$6.95	
	Professional Sales Training	42-4	$7.95	
	Customer Satisfaction: The Other Half of Your Job	57-2	$7.95	
	Managing Disagreement Constructively	41-6	$7.95	
	Professional Excellence for Secretaries	52-1	$6.95	
	Starting A Small Business: A Resource Guide	44-0	$7.95	
	Developing Positive Assertiveness	38-6	$6.95	
	Writing Fitness-Practical Exercises for Better Business Writing	35-1	$7.95	
	An Honest Day's Work: Motivating Employees to Give Their Best	39-4	$6.95	
	Marketing Your Consulting & Professional Services	40-8	$7.95	
	Time Management On The Telephone	53-X	$6.95	
	Training Managers to Train	43-2	$7.95	
	New Employee Orientation	46-7	$6.95	
	The Art of Communicating: Achieving Impact in Business	45-9	$7.95	
	Technical Presentation Skills	55-6	$7.95	
	Plan B: Protecting Your Career from the Winds of Change	48-3	$7.95	
	A Guide To Affirmative Action	54-8	$7.95	
	Memory Skills in Business	56-4	$6.95	

(Continued on next page)

THE FIFTY-MINUTE SERIES
(Continued)

☐ Send volume discount information.

☐ Add my name to CPI's mailing list.

	Amount
Total (from other side)	
Shipping ($1.25 first book, $.50 per title thereafter)	
California Residents add 7% tax	
Total	

Ship to: _____

_____

_____

_____

Phone number: _____

Bill to: _____

_____

_____

_____

P.O. # _____

**All orders except those with a P.O.# must be prepaid.
Call (415) 949-4888 for more information.**

NO POSTAGE
NECESSARY
IF MAILED
IN THE
UNITED STATES

BUSINESS REPLY
FIRST CLASS   PERMIT NO. 884   LOS ALTOS, CA

POSTAGE WILL BE PAID BY ADDRESSEE

Crisp Publications, Inc.
95 First Street
Los Altos, CA 94022

NOTES

NOTES

NOTES

NOTES